Stephen Byrne

Missouri, Kansas and Colorado

A region unsurpassed in the world in its agricultural, mining and manufacturing

prospects

Stephen Byrne

Missouri, Kansas and Colorado
A region unsurpassed in the world in its agricultural, mining and manufacturing prospects

ISBN/EAN: 9783741129810

Manufactured in Europe, USA, Canada, Australia, Japa

Cover: Foto ©Thomas Meinert / pixelio.de

Manufactured and distributed by brebook publishing software (www.brebook.com)

Stephen Byrne

Missouri, Kansas and Colorado

MISSOURI,

KANSAS AND COLORADO.

A REGION UNSURPASSED IN THE WORLD

—IN ITS—

Agricultural, Mining and Manufacturing Resources and Prospects.

DESCRIBED FROM THE LATEST AND BEST AUTHORITIES

—BY—

VERY REV. STEPHEN BYRNE O.S.D.

ST. LOUIS:
PATRICK FOX, CATHOLIC PUBLISHER.
1883.

INTRODUCTION.

THE object of the following description of three of the most promising States of the American Union, is to contribute as far as possible to the elevation of the industrious and dependent poor, to a position of independence at least, if not of wealth.

The English-speaking people of Irish nationality, who form a large part of the present and past emigration to the United States, have hardly given sufficient attention to the study of the great continent to which they are drifting by the million. Yet they will make it their home, and their descendants will do likewise. It is admitted that much has been lost in times past, in the fact of this want of attention to the progress and prospects of our great country. But there is no reason why this should continue, for the opportunities of the present are even better than ever offered before, in these States. The great country, for instance, west of the Mississippi and stretching to the Pacific coast, is just twice as large as that lying between the same river and the Atlantic Ocean, and its development is now only beginning. This vast region comprises 2,000,000 square miles, against 1,000,000 square miles east of the river, leaving out Alaska altogether. When we consider the magnificent agricultural, grazing and mineral resources of this grand country, the idea at once comes home to us that it is indeed the best field for industry and enterprise on the face of the earth. One of the wonders of the age, too, is the railroad system of the United States. It had reached the wonderful figure of 105,000 miles in December, 1882. It was only 35,000 miles in 1865, when the civil war ended. Now we may properly claim 40,000 miles of this grand total, as existing west of the Mississippi. And the yearly increase is so great that we can hardly keep up with it. The chances thus opened for millions of workers on farms on the plains and in the mines, can be more readily imagined than expressed. Yet it is a fact, that out of our fifty millions of people in 1880, only twelve millions, or one-fourth of the total number, were west of the river. In addition to the above facts let us bear in mind also, that this great Western country is divided into States and Territories, each enjoying the full benefit of American law, and each having the right to legislate for itself. Reports of Western lawlessness sometimes set afloat, although not always without foundation, are often grossly exaggerated; and, in fact, outrages against law and order decrease as population and education increase.

The part of this magnificent domain now presented to home-seekers in general, and to English-speaking immigrants and their children in particular, comprises three States of our Union, one of which rests on the Mississippi river as its eastern boundary, and the western limits of another include a large section of the the Rocky Mountains. MISSOURI, KANSAS AND COLORADO constitute the subject of the description now offered to my readers; and they may find it to their advantage to read what is given here as a preparation for more extensive inquiry. No pains have been spared during the last three years to get at the exact facts relating to this region, and the statements put forth are founded on the best authority.

It will be noticed, that the three States described lie nearly within the same degrees of latitude. And they comprise 250,000 square miles of our great domain. The British Islands taken together are not half as large. Neither France nor the German Empire is of equal extent. Their population is now scarcely four millions, and their resources are not one-tenth developed. It is not risking anything to say that their population will be at least fifteen millions in the year 1900.

July 4th, 1883.

MISSOURI.

PART I.

General Description, Statistics of Agriculture, Manufactures, etc., History and Population.

MISSOURI is one of the most prosperous and promising States of the American Union. It takes the first place in population among the States west of the great river Mississippi, Iowa and Texas coming next; and it holds the fifth place among all our States coming next after Illinois. The present population is 2,200,000, instead of 1,700,000 in 1870, and 1,180,000 in 1860. It is entirely within the range of probability that the population of the State will have reached the important figure of four millions in the year 1900. Such progress, present and prospective, deserves the serious attention of all Americans and Europeans who have it in contemplation to seek new homes for themselves and their descendants, or new fields of industry in which their energy and perseverance are most likely to meet with success.

Missouri has a special claim on the attention of immigrants of the Irish and German nationalities, for the reason that their country people are largely represented in this State, and are found in respectable numbers in all classes of society, and in all learned professions in this commonwealth. It has many attractions, too, for all who make profession of the Catholic religion, inasmuch as their Church numbers about 250,000 members here; and is probably better provided than elsewhere in our Union, with religious institutions of all kinds. In proportion to the Catholic population the number of schools, academies, colleges and churches is extraordinary.

Missouri is bounded north by Iowa, east by Illinois and Kentucky, from which it is separated by the Mississippi river; south by Arkansas, and west by Indian Territory, Kansas and Nebraska. It lies between latitudes 36° 30′ and 40° 30′ north, and between longitudes 89° 2′ and 95° 62′ west from London. It is 280 miles long from north to south, and has an average width of 250 miles from east to west. Its area is 65,350 square miles, or 41,826,000 acres, being larger than any State east of the great river and twice as large as Ireland.

No description of Missouri can be complete without taking into account the fact that a marked difference in soil, minerals and general appearance exists in the northern and southern parts of the State. About one-half of the State lies north of the Missouri and Osage rivers, and is similar in most respects to the neighboring State of Iowa. It is a remarkably rich agricultural country; whilst Southern Missouri is equally rich in minerals. The distinction may properly be kept in mind as our description advances: Across the southern part of the State we find the chain of what is called the Ozark Mountains, which in passing east and west renders the face of the country rough and broken, although they scarcely reach 2,000 feet of elevation in any one point. There are large prairies in Southwestern Missouri, but the State, generally, is well timbered. It has the advantage of possessing two of the noblest rivers of North America. The Mississippi, the Father of Waters, constitutes the eastern boundary of the State for a space of 470 miles. It is navigable for the largest river boats between St. Louis and New Orleans. The Missouri, after a course of 2,500 miles, tracing it to its source, touches the northwestern corner of this State, north of St. Joseph, and forms its western boundary, a distance of 250 miles. At Kansas City, on the western border of the State, this noble river takes an easterly course and crosses it in a course of 450 miles. It is navigable not only in Missouri but 2,000 miles beyond the limits of the State.

The Osage is the largest river in the State next to the Missouri, which it joins, after a course of 400 miles, taking its rise in Kansas, and having a general easterly course. It is navigable for small steamboats 200 miles above its mouth. The other principal streams are the Des Moines, the St. Francis, White, Black, Gasconade, Grand and Chariton. These are all navigable in high water.

As to the soil and climate it may be said that about 5,000,000 of acres, lying along the principal streams, cannot be surpassed in fertility in any part of the world. There is no part of the State unfit for successful tillage or pasturage. Southern Missouri is one of the best fruit-countries on our continent. The climate will be understood, when it is stated that from exact calculations, made at St. Louis, for twenty-eight years, it was found that the mean annual temperature was $55\frac{1}{2}°$; and that the lowest mean temperature for any month was $19.3°$ for January, and the highest mean for July $83.5°$.

The actual statistics relating to the productions of the State will fully confirm what has been advanced as to the fertility of the soil. In 1870 it ranked next to Texas and Illinois in cattle, next to Illinois in swine, was fourth in corn and sixth in tobacco, and was next to California in wine.

The number of farms in Missouri, by the census of 1880, was 215,575, against 148,000 in 1870, 92,000 in 1860, and 54,000 in 1850. This steady, regular and rapid increase, as marked in the census years, is worthy of special attention.

The live-stock on farms in 1880 was as follows: Horses, 668,000; mules and asses, 192,000; working oxen, 9,000; milch cows, 661,000; other cattle, 1,410,000; sheep, 1,112,000; hogs, 4,500,000. The increase of the production of Indian corn, in 1880 over that of 1870, was 200 per cent.

In minerals this State is immensely rich. Mining, therefore, is extensively and successfully carried on. Yet we may truly say, that comparing the present condition of mining with what it is likely to be in a few years hence, the business is only now properly commenced. The State professor of Geology, Mr. Swallow, says: "There is no territory on the continent, of equal extent, which contains so many and such large quantities of the most useful minerals as the State of Missouri." Iron ore, of the best quality, is of inexhaustible quantity. The Iron Mountain, for instance, south of St. Louis, is 228 feet high and covers 500 acres at the base, which would give 230 millions of tons above the surface; below the surface it extends indefinitely, giving three millions of tons of ore for every foot of descent. Pilot Knob, another mountain of iron, is 580 feet in height, and covers 360 acres at the base. A large proportion of this huge mass is pure ore. These treasures of the earth were first discovered here in 1720. In 1809, the iron production of the Territory was valued at $40,000. Smelting was commenced in 1824, and there has been a steady increase ever since. Lead mines are also abundant and profitably worked. Copper, zinc, nickel and platinum are found in paying quantities. But, next to iron, the coal deposits of this State are most valuable. In Northern and Western Missouri, coal formations underlie 27,000 square miles, and in some places the veins are found as high as 15 feet thick. Probably 10,000 people are employed in all kinds of mining in this State.

Manufacturing interests at present are mainly

confined to the city of St. Louis and its environs;
but there is a steady increase in this as well as in
all other industrial features of the State in every
part of it. In looking at the map one finds that
Missouri occupies a central position among the
great States of the West and South; that the water
power is splendid; that the raw materials are near
at hand; that the supply of all the necessaries of
life is most abundant; and that, in consequence of
these facts, capital and enterprise will, in course
of time, raise it to the first rank among our
manufacturing States. This will become apparent
by the mere recital of the statistics for 1880, which
are as follows: 8,592 manufacturing establishments; $72,000,000 capital invested; 65,000 hands
employed (of whom 54,000 are over the age of
sixteen years); $24,300,000 paid in wages during
the census year. Value of materials used, $110,-
000,000; value of products, $165,000,000. It may
be remarked that the increase since the census year
is very great.

Closely connected with the farming and manufacturing interests are the railroads of the State. I
need not dwell upon the valuable addition to the
wealth of the country in the fact of about 3,000 miles
of navigable river; but will give in brief the progress and present condition of the railroads. In
February, 1836, the Mayor of St. Louis strongly
recommended the construction of railroads; but his
words seem to have fallen on unwilling or inattentive ears; for we find only 88 miles of railroad in

operation as late as 1853. Twenty years later the number had increased to 2,900 miles; and it is at present (1883) fully 3,500 miles. The completion of the great bridge across the Mississippi, at St. Louis, has given an immense impetus to railroad enterprise in Missouri. It will be borne in mind that every mile of new railroad that is built tends directly to open up and render more valuable the country through which it passes, besides giving employment to those who build it, and keep it in repair; so that, in this respect alone, Missouri of the present time holds out good inducements for working people.

HISTORY AND POPULATION.

Missouri was visited by the celebrated Jesuit priest and missionary explorer Father Marquette, in company with his friend Joliet, in June, 1673. The first settlements were all made by the French, who, in the first half of the eighteenth century constantly passed through this country on their way from Canada to Louisiana. In those days the entire valleys of the St. Lawrence and Mississippi were claimed by the French. The first actual settlement of whites in Missouri was at Ste. Genevieve, in 1735. In 1751, there were only six small settlements within 100 miles of the site of the present city of St. Louis, which was founded in 1764. In 1780 the Indians and English made a terrible attack on St. Louis, and were repulsed with great slaughter. Spain obtained jurisdiction over this part of the country in 1763, and France resumed possession in 1800. In 1803, Missouri, as a part of the Louisiana Territory, was sold by France to the United States; and on the 9th of March, 1804, the flag of the Union first floated over the fort at St. Louis. Missouri was organized as a Territory, in 1812, and was admitted as the twenty-fourth State in the Union, August 10th, 1821.

In 1799 the population of Missouri was only 6,028 souls; in 1820, 66,000; in 1840, 383,000; in 1860, 1,182,000; in 1870, 1,721,000, of whom 118,-000 were free colored; in 1880, 2,168,000, of whom 145,000 were free colored; and 211,600 born in foreign countries. Of these latter 106,000 are reported as having been born in the German Empire; 49,000 in Ireland; 15,800 in England; 8,000 in Canada; 6,000 in Switzerland; 4,600 in France; 3,600 in Scotland, and 3,300 in Bohemia.

The principal cities of Missouri, are:

JEFFERSON CITY, the State capital, on the south bank of the Missouri river, 143 miles from its mouth, and connected with St. Louis and Kansas City by rail. Population, 1880, 5,500.

ST. LOUIS, the sixth city in the United States in population, is situated on the west bank of the Mississippi, 1,378 miles from its mouth. It is near the centre of the great valley of the Mississippi, which comprises nearly 1,300,000 square miles of land, not surpassed on the face of the globe, in variety and abundance of production. This city commands much of the trade of this vast territory;

and is, indeed, a city of much present and prospective greatness. The city extends about fourteen miles along the river, and four miles west of it. St. Louis takes a high rank as a manufacturing city. Among the leading articles of manufacture are: Flour, iron, doors, sashes and blinds, tobacco, white lead and paints. The trade in groceries and dry-goods is immense. The great bridge across the Mississippi, at this point, is indeed one of the wonders of the world. As an object of engineering enterprise it is remarkable even in the United States, which seems to take the lead in works of this kind. The bridge is 2,230 feet long and 54 feet wide. Including the tunnel on the St. Louis side of the river, it cost nine millions of dollars. A dozen railroads have their termini on the Illinois side; and twenty-eight roads, in all, converge towards the city of St. Louis. It is also the centre of 14,000 miles of navigable rivers. The first steamboat arrived in 1817.

The first settlement was made here by the French, of Louisiana and Canada, on the 15th of February, 1764. In 1775, there were 800 inhabitants; in 1830, 7,000; in 1860, 160,773; in 1870, 311,000; and in 1880, 350,318, divided as follows: Males, 179,500 females, 171,000; natives of the United States, 245,500; foreign-born, 105,000; white, 328,-000; colored, 22,250; Chinese, 56.

KANSAS CITY, the second city in the State, is 235 miles west of St. Louis, on the south bank of the Missouri river and on the boundary line between this State and Kansas. The bridge here, across

IN THE GREAT WEST. 15

the Missouri river, is 1,400 feet long, and has cost one million of dollars. Several railroads centre at the Union Depot of Kansas City; and the business of the place increases immensely. The trade is especially large in Texas cattle, and in hogs. The population in 1860, was 4,100; in 1870, 32,260; and in 1880, 55,785, of whom 32,000 were males, and 23,800 females; 46,500 natives, and 9,300 foreign; 47,600 whites, and 8,200 colored. This city promises to be one of the greatest in these States, as it is already among the largest, west of the Mississippi.

ST. JOSEPH is situated on a great bend of the Missouri river, about seventy miles north of Kansas City, and 566 miles from St. Louis, following the river. It contains large flouring and saw mills, pork-packing establishments, and other manufactories. The origin of its importance as a city was, that trains of emigrants used to be formed here, bound for the West. Its population in 1870 was 19,570; in 1880, 32,481, of whom 17,800 were males, and 14,500 females; 26,778 natives, and 5,700 foreign-born; 29,200 whites, and 3,220 colored.

The other principal cities, all ranging from five to twelve thousand in population, are Hannibal, on the Mississippi river, 132 miles north of St. Louis; Springfield, Lexington, Cape Girardeau and St. Charles.

CATHOLIC INTERESTS IN MISSOURI.

The original settlers of this State were all Catholics. There are records and traditions of the priests and missionaries who ministered to the spiritual wants of the first white inhabitants, long before th beginning of this century. To the regular historians of the Church, in these States, we will leave all special investigations and inquiries. Our purpose, is to make known the present condition of the Church in Missouri. The State is divided into an archdiocese and a diocese. The Archdiocese of St. Louis comprises the eastern part of the State, and the Diocese of Kansas City and St. Joseph its western part.

The latest report of the condition of the Archdiocese of St. Louis is as follows:

One archbishop and one bishop; priests, 252; ecclesiastical students, 46; churches, 216; stations and chapels at which Mass is said occasionally, 62; monasteries, 6; convents, 91; seminary, 1; colleges for boys, 4, at which 700 pupils attend; academies for young ladies, 15—attendance at these, 900; industrial schools, 4; orphan asylums, 5; hospitals, 6; asylums, 4. Catholic population, about 175,000.

The united dioceses of Kansas City and St. Joseph make the following report:

One bishop, residing in Kansas City; priests, 70; churches, 75; stations, 60; monasteries, 2; convents with female academies and schools, 14; orphan asylums, 2; hospital, 1. Catholic population, probably 75,000.

In this place I feel it a duty incumbent upon me to mention the fact that, in the American

Catholic Church we can find no names more remarkable, each in its own way, than the names of the distinguished prelates who now guide the destinies of the Church of Missouri. The bare mention of their names is quite sufficient to make this truth known and felt. The great and venerable Archbishop PETER RICHARD KENRICK has watched over the spiritual and temporal interests of his people with zeal, affection and success, during the last forty-two years. His Coadjutor is the renowned Christian orator Bishop P. J. RYAN. Bishop J. J. HOGAN governs Western Missouri with no less zeal, charity and success. He became Bishop of St. Joseph in September, 1868, and was transferred to Kansas City in 1880.

PART II.

Special Description of Places, and Directions for Intending Settlers.

NORTHERN MISSOURI.

AS already noticed, this part of the State, which may be considered as lying north of the Missouri and Osage rivers, comprises some of the best land in the State and in the country. It is generally settled up with a good class of prosperous farmers, and can no longer be said to offer as good inducement to people of limited means as it did a few years ago. Land, improved and unimproved, however, may still be procured on reasonable terms, and in good neighborhoods. Industrious laborers and mechanics are in great demand, and plenty of good chances remain for well-inclined and persevering men. There are so many Catholic congregations in this part of the State, that no Catholic need have any difficulty in making a home among those of his own faith. The sum of one thousand or two thousand dollars is necessary to make a start in this part of the State. There may be exceptions to this; but they are accidental, and not to be counted upon too much.*

*For Northwestern Missouri Father F. W. GRAHAM, of St. Joseph, is excellent authority.

SOUTHERN MISSOURI

May be taken as lying south of the Missouri and Osage rivers. It is about one-half of the State in area. There are thousands of excellent chances for the settlement of the working classes who are industriously inclined, in this part of the State. And the assertion holds good in regard to nearly all of Southern Missouri. Hence, it may be useful to consider this section somewhat in detail.

First, that part of the State lying directly south of St. Louis, along the Mississippi river, is hilly and broken for about one hundred miles. It is full of minerals, as already stated; and much of it is excellent farming and grazing land. It was the first part of the State settled by Europeans; and it is but natural to suppose that the best land has been occupied long ago. But it is still true that good land may be obtained here for from three to fifteen dollars an acre. Going still further south, we enter upon the flat lands below Cape Girardeau. These lie opposite Cairo, Ills., and Western Kentucky. They are of exhaustless fertility and not liable to be worn out by constant tillage. The Rev. F. A. Kleinschnittger, of Charleston, Mississippi County, Mo., is good authority for this part of the State. He will gladly answer all letters of inquiry. The land is not only extraordinarily fertile, producing seventy-five and one hundred bushels of corn to the acre regularly, but it is also exceedingly cheap, ranging from two to fifteen dollars an acre. The great river and the Iron Mountain Railroad furnish easy transportation to this part of the State.

We come now to the description of what may, with full justice, be considered the best part of the State for the industrious working classes of small means. This is emphatically

SOUTH-CENTRAL AND SOUTHWESTERN MISSOURI.

For the sake of convenience we will take the line of the *St. Louis & San Francisco Railroad* first. It is called in this country the "'Frisco" line. It was finished to Rolla, 113 miles southwest of St. Louis in the beginning of the civil war. It has been extended in three directions over 800 miles since then. The very name or title of this road, the "St. Louis & San Francisco Railroad," has a special significance for all of the old religion. It marks two important periods in the settlement by Catholics of the Great West. St. Louis was founded, as already stated, by the French, in 1764, and San Francisco was founded by the Spanish priest, Father Junipero Serra, as an Indian mission, in 1769. The road which, in a few years, will form a link of iron between those two places, now become the greatest cities in the Far West, has, therefore, a peculiar interest for us.

But it is more to the purpose to describe its claims on the attention of intending settlers and emigrants. Most of this road opens up a comparatively new country; for, although settled to a small extent for several years, South-central and

Southwestern Missouri was almost unknown outside of the State itself, until this road was built. Within the last ten or fifteen years prosperous villages and towns have grown up all along its line, and settlers who came poor to these parts have risen to comfort and independence. As proof of this we will give a few details regarding certain counties and towns through which it runs. Franklin County is reached after a ride of thirty miles from St. Louis. This county lies south of the Missouri river, is well watered by streams, which, in course of time, will surely be turned to good account in manufacturing industries. The valleys of these streams are wide and extremely fertile; and the intervening ridges, although high and broken, are admirably adapted to grazing. Sheep, especially, thrive on these hills, and are never known to be diseased. The pasturage is good from March to November. Catholics of Irish and German birth or descent, are very numerous in this county. They possess about fourteen church buildings, and advance steadily in numbers and devotedness. The settlement at Armagh, three miles east of Catawissa station, is worthy of note. It was commenced by Father Patrick Donelly, in 1847. He gave the settlement the name which it still retains, and remained among his people three years. He was a clear-sighted priest, and laid the foundation for the independence and prosperity of the early settlers here, and of their numerous descendants. St. Patrick's Church, at Armagh, is a splendid cut stone building, eighty-eight feet by forty-five, and was completed from its foundation by the present pastor, Rev. E. Berry, in 1863. Father Berry may be truly styled the patriarch of this country; and he is in truth a genuine Catholic priest. Looking from the conical mound near the belfry of St. Patrick's, which is crowned by a statue of Ireland's patron saint, you see the town of Pacific, five miles directly north, in which there is another substantial brick church, also erected by Father Berry. There is a good congregation and an excellent priest, the Rev. Father Feldmann, at this place. Looking eastwardly, we find another church and congregation at Byrnesville, under the direction of the Rev. E. Wynn. It was established also by Father Berry, and is located almost five miles from Armagh. The congregation of Armagh proper furnishes irrefutable proof of the wisdom of those who, in the past or in the present, have made honest efforts to settle the Irish people on the land. No better organized congregation, or better instructed in their religion, can be found anywhere than at Armagh. They are not rich in the general acceptation of the word; but they are contented and independent, healthy and intelligent.

Returning to the station, we pass Moselle, six miles distant, where there is a small settlement of Catholics, mostly German, and very loyal in the practice of their religion. Seventy-one miles from St. Louis, we arrive at Sullivan, where there is a settlement of about sixty Catholic families, attended, like those of Moselle, by the priest of Pacific. There is much cheap land, mostly improved, in the vicinity of Sullivan. Father Feldmann, of Pacific, Mo., will furnish reliable particulars. Leaving Franklin County, we soon arrive at Leasburg, in Crawford County, eighty-three miles from St. Louis. The writer stayed two days here, and was delighted with the conversation and prospects of the settlers whom he met. There are sixteen Irish families here, living, as one of them graphically expressed it, mostly on a circular line, three miles from the station, and surrounding it. There is nothing they all desire more heartily than that the middle part of the circle be soon filled up with Catholics. The land is still cheap, and the prospects of the place excellent. Mr. Patrick Fitzgerald, who occupies a very good farm inside of the circle, half a mile from the depot, has been here fourteen years, and speaks very well of the country. His address is, Leasburg P. O., Crawford County, Mo. He is most willing to give any information to intending settlers. The same is exactly true of Messrs. John O'Brien, William Wallace and William Downs. The last-named gentleman came here lately from another part of the State, and is very well satisfied with his new home. He has a large family, and hopes to provide them all with good homes in this county. He informed the writer that there is government land still open for settlement only a few miles from Leasburg, and that plenty of land can be procured all around for sums ranging between two and seven dollars an acre. It will be borne in mind this is a very healthy region, being the table-land of the Ozark mountain range, over 1,000 feet above the level of the sea. This remark holds good in regard to the whole country 150 miles south and west of this point. A small church is built here, attended from Rolla.

Leaving Leasburg, we soon reach Cuba, ninety miles from St. Louis, and the terminus of a railroad that runs south from this point forty miles, to Salem. It passes through a great iron region; and it is likely to be continued through South Central Missouri, over the Arkansas Line, to Little Rock. Like the road under our immediate consideration, this road, starting at Cuba, opens up another wide field most favorable for settlers. But we must keep Cuba in sight at present. The "'Frisco" Railroad Company own several pieces of good land all around Cuba, which they are willing to dispose of at two dollars an acre. They hold very little land as high as five dollars an acre. The writer met here Mr. Michael Fussmann, a German Catholic, who had lived in Ohio and Indiana; but he prefers this county to either. He occupies 160 acres, of which he "homesteaded" eighty and bought the other eighty at three dollars an acre. Mr. John Fanning lives within three miles of Cuba, and has succeeded very well in farming. He is blessed with a splendid family of good Catholic children, and he has many relatives in the neighborhood. It is properly called the "Fanning Settlement." His information may be thoroughly relied upon. The same is true of Mr. Maurice Dowley, of

Cuba, who keeps store there, and whose information is exact and most truthful in regard to this country. There is a good Catholic church in Cuba, in which Mass is said occasionally by Father P. O'Loughlin, of Rolla. The congregation advances steadily in numbers and fervor.

We now advance along our "'Frisco" line to Knob View, where we find a few Irish families, and then to St. James, in which an elegant little church exists, and the beginning of an excellent congregation, consisting in about equal numbers of Irish and German people. This village, of about 500 inhabitants, is 13 miles from Cuba and 103 miles from St. Louis. What has been said regarding the advantages for settlers at the former town, applies with equal or even greater force to St. James and its vicinity. Many thousand acres of land, improved and unimproved, are for sale cheap in all directions. Mr. William James is a prominent citizen of this place, and has, in a great measure, built it up. He is indeed a worthy man, and a true friend of the working classes. He takes the deepest interest in helping them to locate on good land, and hundreds have benefited by his advice. Mr. George T. Bacon is Mr. James' agent and bookkeeper. He is also in the real estate business, and has for sale farms ranging in size from forty acres (near the town) to 600 acres of prairie and timber land, about twelve miles from the depot. The Meramec Iron Company, of which these two gentlemen are representatives, hold about 12,000 acres of land, consisting of farms

of all sizes, and varying in distance from the depot
from three to ten miles. Full and reliable information will be given by addressing either of these gentlemen, personally or by letter. St. James is located
in the eastern part of Phelps County. The writer
has spoken to several farmers of this vicinity, and
their testimony regarding the country is unanimously
favorable. He would greatly rejoice in a large in-
flow of people into this country. Ten miles west we
come to the beautiful little town of

ROLLA,

So much spoken of in the time of the late war, as
the terminus of the railroad now under consideration and the centre of supplies for the army operat-
ing in this part of the State. It is at present an
elegantly located town of at least 2,000 people. It is
the site of the School of Mines, a branch of the State
University, and of a most flourishing flouring mill,
which is operated by Mr. Joseph Campbell, a native
of Ireland, and a most reliable gentleman in all
that relates to this part of the State. The oldest
Catholic church within a radius of seventy-five
miles is also located here. It bears the name of
St. Patrick, and was erected in 1861. There is
also a pastoral residence, which is the home of the
devoted missionary priest of this region, Rev. P.
O'Loughlin, already mentioned. But it is his
place of residence not more than half the time, for he
has charge of six counties and about twelve chapels
and stations in all directions. No one is more

willing to impart the most valuable information regarding this country, than Father O'Loughlin. He is able to corroborate the statements already made in this report; and what has been written in regard to the other localities is more than true, as applied to Rolla and its vicinity.

One of the most intelligent gentlemen met by the writer has his principal office here. It is Mr. F. E. Dowd, agent for the sale of the railroad and other lands in all this country. Mr. Dowd is indeed a most reliable gentleman, and his honesty and success in his line of business are well known. I subjoin a few items furnished by him for this pamphlet:

"Phelps and the adjoining counties are unsurpassed for the production of fruits as regard both quality and quantity. Two large Aulden fruit evaporators will be erected in Rolla this fall, giving additional value to small fruit culture. This whole section of the State has been designated the 'Fruit Basket of Missouri.'

"The county is also admirably adapted to stock-raising, having twelve to fifteen running streams and innumerable springs of pure water. The valleys and hillsides are covered with a rich growth of nutritious grasses, on which cattle can subsist from March until December, with little expense to the owner, except an occasional salting. Rolla is only 113 miles from the great cattle market of St. Louis, so that the business becomes more and more profitable.

"The best wheat of the State is raised in this county, and much of it turned into flour at Rolla. Hence, the market is at the door of the grower, and the production of the county last year (1882) was 500,000 bushels.

"Mineral industries are yet in their infancy here. Iron, lead and fire-clay are the principal mining industries. Of fire-clay the quantity is unlimited and the quality unsurpassed.

"The climate is healthy, free from the extremes of heat and cold. The winters are short and mild; the summers are long, but not oppressive. Rolla is 1,100 feet above the level of the sea.

"Within the past five years over 500 families have made locations and settlements in this vicinity."

Mr. Dowd has hundreds of farms for sale, at all prices between two and fifteen dollars an acre. He is most willing to describe them by letter, or show them to the intending settler, which is always preferable. I spoke to several farmers and old residents of this place of the Irish nationality. They all agreed in giving a good account of the country. Many are coming here from Illinois, Indiana and Wisconsin, and find this country superior in many respects to that in which they had lived for years. The healthfulness of the climate and the cheapness of the land form the principal attractions. The reader will especially note the two addresses of Rev. P. O'Loughlin and Mr. F. E. Dowd, Rolla, Mo.

To avoid being tedious, we will rapidly pass the

beautiful Gasconade river at Jerome, and several other stations, the description of which would be little more than a repetition of what has been already written, and halt at Lebanon, the elegant and thriving county seat of Laclede County, numbering about 2,500 people, and distant 185 miles from St. Louis. The writer met here many old acquaintances, known years ago on the Southern railroads. But they had given up public works at last, and are now become prosperous and independent farmers. Many of these commenced with little else than a team of horses or oxen, ten to fifteen years ago, and are now worth from three thousand to seven thousand dollars each. There are many inducements for our people to settle in and near Lebanon; but the principal are a good church and a most devoted priest, Rev. E. J. Sheeby, who will leave nothing undone, to direct properly all intending settlers; also a healthy climate and fertile lands very cheap, in all directions. The Catholics of Lebanon, under Father Sheeby's leadership, have formed an immigration society, for the very purpose of assisting and advising those of their creed who may cast their eyes this way, to make good selections. Lebanon, is near the summit of the Ozark region, but the land here is not broken, as a rule. It is a tableland, and easily cultivated. Mr. H. Attaway, of the Laclede Hotel and Mr. Hannegan, are also good authorities regarding this country, and most willing to answer letters of inquiry.

We now take the train again, and pass several

stations, the most remarkable of which is Marshfield, 216 miles from St. Louis, and said to be the highest ground in the State. It is 1,600 feet above the level of the sea. Leaving this place, we pass down the southwestern slope of the Ozark range, and begin to see the beautiful varieties of prairie and wooded land intermingled, which forms a special characteristic of all this part of Missouri, as far as the boundary lines of Kansas and Indian Territory. At the distance of 240 miles southwest of St. Louis we arrive at North Springfield, a thriving and busy suburb of Springfield, and the location of the car and repair works of the St. Louis & San Francisco road. These works and the buildings connected with them, occupy eighty acres of ground, and give employment to at least 250 men. All the repairing and construction required for nearly 900 miles of road, is done here. Most of the hands employed are of Irish birth or descent, and they have built an excellent brick church, 70 feet by 36, a short distance from the depot. No better men in the matter of industry, sobriety and attention to their families and to their religion, can be found generally, than those of North Springfield.

The public square of Springfield proper, is about a mile and a half from the depot at this place, and they are connected by street cars. This old Springfield is a most flourishing little city, and elegantly located. It was celebrated in the late civil war as being in the neighborhood of the battle of Wilson's

Creek, at which the Federal Gen'l Lyon was killed. This was on the 9th of August, 1861; but no traces of these bloody scenes now remain, save the Federal and Confederate cemeteries near the city, which are well kept, especially the former, and decorated every year. Springfield has good flouring mills, which are able to turn out 700 barrels of flour a day; also a cotton mill, employing 100 hands, and a woolen mill, employing forty hands. There are wagon shops and other works, all doing a good business. The Drury College is here, and is located very beautifully about midway between the two Springfields, which are fast growing into one city, and contain together about 12,000 people. The Catholic Church of old Springfield has been most worthily presided over by Rev. Theodore Kussmann, for the last ten years. A splendid new church is in course of erection, and the Sisters of Loretto conduct an academy and school. The priest of North Springfield is the Rev. J. F. O'Neill, who is most devoted to his duties, and most willing to direct wisely, all who may desire his advice. Father Kussmann is a most excellent guide too, and is particularly interested in the settlement of Catholics of Eastern States who may be inclined hitherward. Western people are of course supposed to know the country better than those of the East. Springfield is acknowledged to be the capital of Southwestern Missouri, and this fact will be doubly established, when the great railroad now in course of construction between Kansas

City and Memphis, Tenn., and passing through Springfield, will have been completed. This result is only the work of a few months, and then Springfield will be united in business interests with the great cotton mart of Memphis, which is 280 miles distant. Kansas City is 200 miles from this point, so that the whole road is nearly 500 miles long. It is most important to bear in mind, that the part of it running to Memphis opens for settlement almost an entirely new country, in which there is a large quantity of government land for sale or settlement on the homestead principle. There are splendid opportunities in this' region at present for well-inclined workers. The president of this new road is Mr. G. H. Nettleton, of Kansas City, who will gladly give all particulars about land and transportation.

Coming back to the depot at North Springfield, we again resume our journey on the 'Frisco line, and arrive at Plymouth, which is 285 miles from St. Louis. A branch road runs directly south from this point to Fort Smith, Arkansas, 134 miles distant. This makes the whole distance from St. Louis to Fort Smith exactly 419 miles. The development of new country involved in this new branch I will not describe, but it can be readily understood by all thoughtful men. The celebrated Eureka Springs, of Arkansas, are reached by this branch of the road. Returning to Plymouth, we soon reach Peirce City, five miles distant from which the Kansas Division of our great 'Frisco line takes its departure. This branch is 243 miles long, and brings you through a splendid country, mostly prairie and partly wooded. You pass through the beautiful and thriving cities of Carthage, and Joplin, which is celebrated for its zinc and lead works; and soon pass over the Kansas line, on your way to Halstead, in Southeastern Kansas, the terminus of this branch. There are Catholic churches and resident priests at Pierce City, Carthage and Joplin. Scarcely, in the United States, do we find more desirable locations for settlement than in this splendid new country. Returning to Pierce City, we again take the main line of the road and pass through Neosho, Dayton and Seneca, on the line of the Indian Territory. Then Vinita is reached, which is a village of the Indian Nation, and the point at which our road is crossed by the Missouri, Kansas & Texas Railroad, which brings you to Dallas, Tex. and all points of that great and growing State. Vinita is 364 miles from St. Louis, and Tulsa, fifty-four miles further west, or 428 miles from the same city, is the terminus of the main line of the St. Louis & San Francisco (or 'Frisco) Railroad.

It will be seen that in dwelling so long on this special road occasion has been furnished to explain more fully the condition and prospects of South Central and Southwestern Missouri, which I ventured to assert in the beginning was the best field in the State at present for emigrants and settlers. All further particulars will be cheerfully furnished by addressing Capt. C. W. ROGERS, General Manager of this road, or Mr. D. WISHART, General Ticket Agent, St. Louis, Missouri. Capt. Rogers is indeed a most practical and reliable gentleman, and will use all reasonable efforts to accommodate all with whom he has dealings.

In conclusion, I may say that, if 50,000 families of our people were now located in Southern and Western Missouri alone, it would be well for them and for the State too. It is a country not one third populated nor one-fourth developed. Its greatest riches to-day, would be the inflowing of thousands of industrious people. And be it steadily borne in mind, that the chances here offered to rich men and capitalists are even better, in proportion to their means, than the chances awaiting the poorer classes. Farming, grazing and mining on a large scale, may be safely entered into in any part of this country.

If I deal lightly with other parts of the State it is because they are better known than this, and especially because the best chances for the largest number whom I expect to reach by these writings, no longer exist as a rule in Northern Missouri.

Be it strictly remembered that, there is no richer country on the whole continent in iron ore, in lead, zince and copper, than the part of Missouri which I have endeavored briefly to describe. The advancement of the country as time goes on, in all these industries is indeed incalculable.

KANSAS.

THIS is a great and growing State of the West that is likely to survive the exaggerations of friends and enemies; for, of all other Western States I know of none which has received such unmitigated praise and such unqualified abuse. Both the one and the other have come, no doubt, from the respective feelings evoked by success or disappointment. It will be our duty, in this outline, as far as possible, to avoid both extremes, and give the truth so far as our own means of information warrant it. I may remark in the outset, that I have it on excellent authority that, in the single year 1878, 200,000 persons, young and old, are known to have sought homes in this State. Such being the case, it is not probable that we are to follow the accounts sometimes given from the reflection of the dark side of the picture.

GENERAL DESCRIPTION.

Kansas is bounded on the north by Nebraska, on the east by Missouri, south by the Indian Territory, and west by Colorado. It lies between latitudes 37° and 40° north, and between longitudes 94° 40′ and 102° west from London. It is 410 miles long from east to west, and 210 miles wide from north to south. The area is 81,318 square miles, or 53,043,520 acres.

Kansas has no mountains or even high hills, but is a gently undulating prairie, presenting a constant succession of rolling elevations and valleys. The rise from east to west is about six feet in the mile; the elevation on the eastern border is about 750 feet above the level of the sea; and at the western boundary line of the State, 4,000 feet. The principal rivers are as follows: The Kansas, which traverses the State from west to east, with its principal tributary the Smoky Hill Fork, enters the Missouri at Kansas City. The Republican Fork, 400 miles long, is another of its branches. The great river Missouri, which is, we may say, the common property of many States and Territories, forms the eastern boundary of Kansas for a distance of eighty miles. The Arkansas river, rising in the Rocky Mountains, has a winding course of 500 miles in this State.

SOIL, CLIMATE, PRODUCTIONS.

Most of the soil, especially in the eastern and central part of the State, is of great fertility, having a depth of from one to ten feet. The soil in the western part of the State is lighter. So great is the growth of prairie grass, that it is sometimes high enough to conceal a man on horseback. What is called the "buffalo grass," is short; and is considered especially good for the fattening of cattle.

The changes of the temperature are great and sudden; but, as a rule, the summers are long and temperate, and the winters short and dry. The thermometer rarely reaches zero in winter; and sometimes reaches ninety-seven degrees of heat in summer. In this particular and in all others pertaining to Kansas, I invite special attention to the letters and statistics at the end of this article.

The staple productions are corn, wheat, oats, rye, potatoes and tobacco. There is a constant annual increase in all these productions; and the State advances rapidly in wealth and promise. The numerous streams of Kansas furnish abundant water-power, and great inducements to manufacturers; but, at present, the cultivation of the soil is the principal occupation of the people. Coal underlies 17,000 square miles of the whole surface of the State; and its veins have been found to be from one to seven feet thick. Salt is also found in large quantities.

RAILROADS.

The railroad system of this State is very complete, and forms an important feature of the country. These roads have grants of land from the government, which they sell on very favorable terms, as to rates and time. I refer in a special manner to the valuable letter of Bishop Fink, in this particular. In 1865, Kansas had only 40 miles of railroad; in 1873, 2,400; in 1880, about 3,500.

HISTORY AND POPULATION.

The valley of the Kansas was visited in 1719, by M. Dustine, a French officer, sent out by Bienville, Governor of Louisiana, on a tour of discovery in the interests of trade with the native Indians. More than a century elapsed before any practical steps were taken to colonize the country. Kansas forms a part of the vast territory ceded by the well-known treaty of 1803, when the Louisiana purchase was negotiated between this country and France.

When Kansas was about to become a State, much trouble arose between the people of the northern and southern sections of the United States, as to whether it would come into the Union as a slave or a free State. In truth, we may trace the immediate occasion of the civil war of 1861-65, to the warm and sometimes bloody quarrels growing out of this controversy. From both parties large numbers of persons were sent into the Territory, not so much for permanent and peaceful settlement, as to uphold the ascendancy of their respective sides in the political situation. At last two separate governments were formed, and a state of civil strife ensued. We need not enter into details; these will be found in the general history of the country. But at length the Constitution adopted at Wyandotte, prohibiting slavery, was accepted by Congress;. and Kansas was admitted as the thirty-fourth State, January 29th, 1861.

POPULATION.

In 1854, no settlement of whites existed in Kansas. Excepting the soldiers of the United States' forts, the Indians held undivided possession of this splendid hunting ground. In that year it became a Territory, and settlers began to move into it very rapidly. In 1855 the population was 8,500; in 1860, 107,000; in 1870, 364,700; in 1880, 996,000; divided as follows: Males, 537,000; females, 459,000; natives of the United States, 386,000; foreign-born, 108,000; whites, 952,000 and colored 44,000. Of the foreign-born, there were 28,000 Germans, 15,000 Irish, 14,000 English, 12,000 Canadians and 11,000 Swedes.

The capital city is Topeka, on the south side of the Kansas river; population, 15,450. Leavenworth is a flourishing city of 16,600 people, on the west bank of the Missouri. Atchison, on the same river, has 15,100 people, according to the late census. Lawrence, Fort Scott, etc.. are flourishing cities.

NOTE.—From the U. S. report, I take the following statistics of agriculture and manufacture for the year 1880: Number of farms, 138,561 (in 1870, 38,302, and in 1860, 10,400). Live stock on farms in 1880: Horses, 431,600; mules and asses, 65,000; working oxen, 17,000; milch cows, 418,000; other cattle, 1,016,000; sheep, 500,000; swine, 1,788,000. Five and one-half times as much corn was raised in Kansas in 1880, as in 1870.

Manufactures in this State, in 1880, are reported as follows: Establishments, 2,803; capital employed, $11,200,000; hands engaged, 12,040; wages paid, $4,000,000; value of materials used, $21,000,000; value of productions, $31,000,000. The water power in this State is excellent and the manufacturing outlook good.

OPPORTUNITIES FOR SETTLEMENT IN KANSAS.

Under this head I have concluded, from a long and careful study of the subject, that they are excellent. Some, of course, are constantly telling us that if we allow the present to slip from our hands, in the matter of procuring Western farms, no chance will remain any longer. This, as I conceive, is a mistake. As long as unimproved land can be had for from three to seven dollars an acre, on a credit of eight or ten years, the chances may be considered very good. Not only is this the case, but improved farms—that is, those partially cultivated, and having upon them a dwelling of some kind, together with a barn, etc., may be obtained in large numbers in almost all the counties in Kansas, for ten dollars an acre and less. This is just two pounds in British money. The prices of land in Kansas were higher ten years ago than they are now; and for two reasons: first, because the currency of the United States is now on the basis of gold; and secondly, because the lands of Kansas were then held in large quantities by railroad companies and speculators, who have found it greatly to their advantage to sell out, lest they should be ruined by taxes on their unproductive real estate. All this turns to the advantage of the poor man; and hence the large tide of emigration lately, turning in this direction.

RELIGIOUS AND EDUCATIONAL OPPORTUNITIES.

It may be safely asserted that there is not a single State in the Union where more honest efforts have been made by the Catholic clergy, bishops and priests, to encourage and elevate their people than in Kansas. They have taken pains also to induce immigration into this fertile State. Bishops Miége and Fink, Fathers Swemberge, Pichler, Bononcini, and a great number of other devoted priests, have left nothing undone, by which to benefit their co-religionists. True, their efforts have not been carried on upon so large a scale as those of Bishop Ireland, in Minnesota; but substantial and successful work in the matter of colonization has been done in Kansas. The supply of educational institutions, both male and female, especially in the eastern part of the State, is most creditable to all concerned. In the Catholic Almanac of 1882, we find the following: 1 bishop, residing in Leavenworth; 94 priests, and 17 clerical students; 148 churches and chapels; 6 religious communities of men, and 5 of women; 3 colleges and 3 academies. Catholic population, about 80,000.

SPLENDID AND VALUABLE LETTER OF BISHOP FINK, OF LEAVENWORTH, KAS.

The following most practical and useful letter was addressed in the fall of 1880, by Bishop Fink to Father Byrne, to be inserted in his forthcoming book on the Great West as the home for immigrants. It is so carefully prepared and so replete with good advice to working people seeking homes in the West, that its perusal is sure to benefit many of our readers. Much has been said for and against Kansas, but all sensible people will bear in mind that a State which had only 364,000 people in 1870, and in 1880 has 1,000,000—that is, nearly three times the population of 1870—must have in it something worth knowing:

VERY REV. AND DEAR FATHER BYRNE:—It is with great pleasure 1 have learned that you are about publishing a new book which is to furnish reliable information for immigrants. Allow me to send you some items in regard to my own State.

Every one of the great Western States and Territories has its millions of acres of land for occupation by immigrants; every one of them has its own advantages, and offers special inducements; but Kansas, I think, offers more than any other.

Kansas lies far enough south to be free from severe winters. We have a few days now and then during the winter season which are cold; however, stock-raisers leave their cattle out without shelter all winter, particularly, in the southern part of the State; and very rarely any damage is suffered thereby.

The lands are uniformly very productive; the black soil being from two to ten feet deep, everything can be grown except products peculiar to the tropical climate. From the agricultural census of '78, I copy the wheat grown in Kansas as compared with Ohio.

In 1866, Ohio produced 10,208,854 bushels of wheat.
In 1866, Kansas produced 260,455 bushels of wheat.
In 1877, Ohio produced 26,000,000 bushels of wheat.
In 1877, Kansas produced 14,316,000 bushels of wheat.
In 1878, Ohio produced 16,000,000 bushels of wheat.
In 1878, Kansas produced 32,315,358 bushels of wheat.

This is to say, that the wheat yield of Kansas in 1878, was more than double that of Ohio, which is one of the best agricultural States. Now, when we consider that Ohio is an old State, whose lands have been under cultivation for a number of years, and that its population in '78 was about three times that of Kansas, the difference is astonishing. What the wheat yield of Kansas will be when the millions of acres of waste land shall have been cultivated by industrious farmers, almost surpasses calculation. As is the wheat yield, so is that of other agricultural products.

Water is plentiful and of excellent quality.

Like all other prairie States, Kansas has not much timber, except along the rivers and creeks.

Coal is in great abundance, particularly in the eastern part of the State.

The State is traversed by railroads in all directions; new lines are being projected and built still. By this means the State is rendered easy of access, almost to its most remote parts. People have market facilities, and the ordinary conveniences of life are within reach of the new settlers.

In most parts of the State is found rock for building purposes, which proves to be of great advantage to the immigrant.

The population of the State, which, according to the U. S. census of 1870, was 364,000, has now reached nearly one million. The Catholics number about 75,000 to 80,000 souls, with about 120 churches, attended by about eighty priests. In all congregations sufficiently large, Catholic schools have been established, which are mostly under the direction of Sisters.

The higher educational affairs are conducted by three colleges and the same number of academies.

The facilities for getting a home are very encouraging. Our railroads, which run through the best portions of the State, sell their lands at very reasonable figures, from two dollars to about six dollars, on an average.

The sales are on long time, generally eleven years. In the first year nothing is asked except the interest, at the rate of seven per cent.; in every other year, one-tenth, with interest. For cash within one or two years, a deduction of about one-fourth to one-eighth on purchase is allowed. By this arrangement, land sold for instance, for $4.00 an acre, costs actually, only from $2.75 to $3.00

Who should settle in Kansas.—Parties desirous of settling on land in Kansas, should first of all be good Catholics, who wish to establish a home for themselves and their children, and at the same time are sincerely desirous to get to heaven. They should be willing to learn something of our State, as every State has peculiarities of its own. If immigrants are not willing to pay heed to these at the start, they generally have to pay dear enough for it in course of time. They should be possessed of some means, say $400 to $500, and begin on a small scale. Many have come into the State with no means whatever, who are well-to-do now; but as too many risks are to be run by such immigrants, I would not wish to advise it.

How to locate.—Either as colonies or by single families.

If colonies are formed, which take up a large body of land at once, the railroad companies sell their lands a good deal cheaper, and give special rates for passengers and freight. If by single families, it is advisable that one of the family come first to look up the land, and only after some little preparation shall have been made, the family itself should follow. By following this advice, a good deal of expense is saved and many other difficulties are avoided.

When to come to look up the lands.—Any time during the year, except winter.

When to immigrate.—The best time is February, as the immigrant can plant enough of a spring crop to support him through next winter, and enable him to break up land for putting in a fall crop. In other and more northern States, I am told, immigrants have to support themselves for twelve to eighteen months before getting a support from their lands. In Kansas, it is ordinarily not over six months.

Where to locate.—Immigrants coming by single families or as individuals, who have very limited means, should rather settle in places that have been settled for some time, and which have enough of vacant lands around them. Such immigrants should *rent* on shares for a few years, until they will be able to buy a piece of land with the money they have already earned. A certain number of families can find very superior advantages by this means of proceeding, in almost every Catholic settlement. In time of need they will be spared a deal of unnecessary suffering. Immigrants coming in a colony, should select the lands—fix the price for same—and as soon as this has been accomplished, each man should pay for his own land himself, as he may be able, and get the deed directly from the railroad company, instead of the colony. It would be too tedious to give here the reasons for this advice, but the advantages are many, and the disadvantages of this system are unknown to me.

Dangers immigrants are apt to incur.—As the rainfall in our State follows the cultivation of the soil, immigrants should not venture too far west. I would advise them not to go further west than about 250 miles from the eastern line of the State; they are apt not to have the necessary rainfall west of that line, at least at present and for several years to come. There are millions of acres of fine and cheap lands this side of that line. No immigrant should spend any more money on improvements than the necessity of the case may require, at the start, till he shall have earned some. In all new States, the interest on money is too high, and cannot be had. A little cash laid up for emergencies, is a very desirable thing for the new comer.

As but very few people that wish to come to Kansas have the means to travel over the whole State to find suitable homes, I will give the names and directions of several of our good priests of the diocese, in whose districts there are large tracts of land that can be had at very reasonable figures, and in whose vicinity they will find a church, and in the course of a few years, also a Catholic school. In connection with this I desire to state that parties may address the undersigned, stating what means they have, if married or single, and such other circumstances as may be necessary to enable me to direct them to proper places.

Parties desirous of locating in the northern and northwestern districts, may apply to Rev. Emmanuel Hartig or Rev. Father Timothy, Seneca, Kan.; Rev. John Pichler, at Hanover, Kan.; Rev. B. Hudson, Frankfort, Kan.; Rev. Father Frederick, Beloit, Kan.; Thomas Bartl, Seneca, Kan.

Parties wishing to locate in the central portion of the State, address: Reverends John Begley, at Effingham, Kan.; F. M. Hayden, Solomon City, Kan.; P. Maurer, Salina, Kan. Parties desirous of securing homes in the southern and southwestern portions of the State, will obtain reliable information and good advice from the following reverend pastors:

Revs. Michael Casey, at Olathe, Kan.; Daniel Hurley, Paola, Kan.; F. T. Wattron, Fort Scott, Kan.; Father Cyril Knoll, O.C.C., Scipio, Kan.; Jesuit Fathers, at Osage Mission, Kan.; P. Scholl, Independence, Kan.; C. L. Kearful, Humboldt, Kan.; Jos. Perrier, Emporia, Kan.; Felix P. Sweinbergh, Newton, Kan.; G. M. Kelly, Winfield, Kan.

I remarked that Kansas offers more real advantages and less disadvantages to the industrious immigrant, than any other of the new States or Territories with which I am acquainted. However, no one should be led to think that the paradise of old is located in our State, and that he will find no difficulties at all. There was a serpent even in Paradise, and the immigrants will meet with difficulties too. In some years these new States have not enough of rainfall. Some of our neighboring Territories raise a species of tramps, called grasshoppers. As long as these fellows have enough to eat at home, they do not trouble their neighbors; but when their food is scant, they overrun the neighboring Territories in search of it, and Minnesota, Western Iowa, Dakotah, Nebraska, and last of all, even our Kansas, are invaded, which, however, happens but seldom.

Now, Dear Father, please excuse the many shortcomings you may find in these lines. I hope, however, that I have said enough to enable those who may read this letter to form an intelligent opinion as to the general features of the State. Now, may God bless your forthcoming work and these lines, so that His kingdom on earth may increase, many now poor families may find that support which will enable them to serve God with so much more fervor and less concern about their daily necessities, and believe me to be*

Yours very respectfully,
† LOUIS M. FINK, O. S. B.,
Bishop of Leavenworth.

The following letter, which I heartily recommend to the perusal of my readers, is from the Rev. J. Pichler, himself, a pioneer in the great cause of Catholic Colonization, and a very successful one; therefore his words are of the greatest value:

HANOVER, WASHINGTON CO., KAN.
January, 1880.

DEAR FATHER BYRNE:—I lately read in the *Catholic Review*, a letter addressed by you to the Western clergy

---

* JULY, 1883.—It is indeed consoling to know, that although nearly three years have elapsed since the above was written, the good Bishop has not found it necessary to make any material change in the statements then put forth.

But what is most cheering is the fact that in April of this year (1883) a central Immigration society has been established at Leavenworth, under the control and direction of Bishop Fink. Branch societies having the same object, are established in all Catholic settlements of the State, and a mighty work for the poor immigrant and settler is soon to be accomplished. If you have a mind to see the latest directions, send to VERY REV. I. F. CUNNINGHAM, Leavenworth, Kas., for a copy of the last pamphlet enclosing a three-cent stamp.—S. B.

of certain States, requesting detailed information, facts and facilities for Catholic immigration. Success to you, dear Father; and success to all who engage in that most timely and charitable enterprise. As a Western missionary for twelve years, I have always been an advocate, more or less, and, as far as I could, a promoter of emigration. Eighteen months ago I visited the East, in that cause; and was last St. Patrick's day, in Chicago, as a delegate to the Catholic Colonization Convention. I have gained over to the purer and freer life on Western lands, one hundred families; and I must say that all who have exchanged city drudgery for country independence, could not be induced to go back if you gave them a mansion on Wall street. After this brief preface, permit me to present my special claims for colonization in Kansas.

First of all, Kansas is free from the extremes of heat and cold felt in other places. The winters are milder and shorter than in States farther north; the heat is not so intense as in the Southern States. The climate is therefore more genial and healthy, because the air is dry and free from malaria, chills and fevers. The soil is rich and most conducive to the production of all kinds of grain; it also produces rich nutritious grasses, affording a free pasture to cattle, sheep, horses, etc. No fences are required, by reason of the herd law, which saves to a poor new beginner both time and money—both very desirable for one just arrived. The land is cheap, selling from $3.00 to $6.00 an acre, and most of it on long time with a low rate of interest. Mark this: improved farms may easily be had at from $1,000 to $1,500 for 160 acres, in various places near me. These have already upon them houses, stables, barns, orchards, etc.; and it is often more desirable for even a poor man, if he has a little means, to buy them, than to face a raw tract of land. We have fire-wood here at from $3.50 to $4.00 a cord; there is a good market also, for the St. Joseph & Western R. R., is running through the northern part of the county; and the Chicago, Burlington & U. P. R. R., runs through the centre of the county. As to church facilities, we have five Catholic churches in the county. The largest and most prosperous is at Hanover, in the northeastern part of the county, where there is also a school and a resident pastor—myself, at this time. Within from two to seven miles of Hanover, there is plenty of room for 200 families yet; and even, if that addition were made to our population, it would still be quite sparse compared with the Eastern States. True there is no longer any

homestead land here; but many prefer to pay the small sum required, rather than go to the Western frontier and get lands for nothing. But pay strict attention to my last words: Let no amateur farmer come here. We do not want "book" farmers or political dreamers; for, to use a Western expression: "They won't make it go." It takes much industry, frugality and perseverance, a moderate knowledge of farming, and a little capital, to insure success. I shall be always happy if these few lines may induce some poor struggling people to become independent. Any further information, if desired, will be cheerfully given, by
Yours most respectfully,
REV. J. PICHLER.

It will interest our readers to peruse the following letter, written from the same place this year, 1883. It is well to see how one corroborates the other, the difference of time being considered:

HANOVER, WASHINGTON CO., KAN.,
April, 1883.
EDITOR OF THE PILOT.—The Rt. Rev. Bishop L. Fink, O. S. B., of Leavenworth, and his ninety-four priests have lately organized themselves into a board of immigration, with branch committees in every congregation, consisting of the pastor and three competent laymen in each, to promote the interests of those that intend coming West. Their object is not to stir up such as may enjoy a certain comfort and ease at their present homes, but to direct and counsel the homeless, or those that are tired of home and have already made up their minds to seek a new berth in the great West, without knowing exactly how, when and where, lest in the rush of their westward march they become estranged from, or even lost to the mother Church. Such a branch committee has now been established at this place, with the Rev. John Pichler at its head, who, by his activity and zeal in this matter, is a power in himself. Among the readers of THE PILOT, there may be more or less persons falling within the class above described; and to such it might be welcome news to hear that we have here a sort of Catholic headquarters, with a substantial stone church (50x100), a two-story school building of solid stone (40x64), and a like parsonage, all new and clear of debt. The congregation

numbers 200 families, Irish, German and Bohemian, mostly farmers; and there being room for more, with good and cheap land at from $6.00 to $12.00 per acre, within a few miles from town and church, a healthy climate, a rich soil, especially adapted to stock breeding, but equally good for all the ordinary farm products. We would call the attention of the new comers to the fact that the church fabric being in running order, little or no co-operation will be required of them in this line, which only those can fully appreciate who, in spite of difficulties of every kind, have succeeded to build up a home for themselves, and by the aid of their zealous pastor, a permanent place of worship for their children. The advantages which this section can hold out to the industrious settler are manifold, and will, with your permission, be brought before your readers in short sketches from time to time. Meanwhile anyone may address the undersigned, or better still, the Rev. J. Pichler, who is ever ready to give information. To-day we might mention the rare chance offering to any competent man with a moderate capital, in opening a slaughter and packing house on a small scale in this town; considering the many carloads of hogs that are shipped, week after week, to St. Joseph, Mo., and of which a good portion comes back again in the shape of hams, etc. But more anon.

By authority of the Committee,
A. I. IANSENIUS, M. D.,
Practicing Physician.

The following letter is from a worthy priest in Southeastern Kansas, and may be thoroughly relied upon. Like its predecessor, it contains most valuable information, for which we heartily thank the reverend writer:

SCAMMONSVILLE, KANSAS,
February 18th, 1880.

REV. STEPHEN BYRNE, NEWARK.

ESTEEMED FATHER PROVINCIAL:—In response to your inquiry, I send you a condensed account of my Missions:

My district takes in the southeast corner of the State of Kansas. I have charge of Cherokee County, one-half of Labette and a part of Crawford counties.

When I came here, I found a brick church at Baxter Springs, built in 1870, by Rev. J. M. Doherty, and a small wooden chapel near my present residence, built in 1879, by Rev. F. Colleton, S. J. I took charge of these missions at the close of 1872, and since then I have built commodious frame churches here near Scammonsville, and at Empire City (Cherokee County), at Chetopa and at Oswego (Labette County), and, finally, at Girard (Crawford County.)

This county and that of Crawford contain the famous "Joy land," the price of which has formerly been held too high for the poor settlers, but lately has been so reduced as to bring it within the reach of everyone. They are buying right along, and it averages $3.50 per acre. There is considerable mining of soft coal going on in this neighborhood; a circumstance which, added to the good market afforded by competing railroads, makes this corner of Kansas a very desirable spot for emigrants. The land is generally very good and productive of rich harvests of corn, wheat, flax, castor beans, etc.

In Labette County, coal is also to be found, and some of its land is the best I have ever seen. Most of the good land is occupied; but farms with more or less improvements can be bought at $7.00 per acre and upwards. The proximity to the Indian Territory does not impair in the least the security of the settlers, for the Indians that live in it are civilized and peaceable. It will rather improve the market for produce, as soon as it is open for settlement, which will happen in the near future.

This is the plain truth, without boasting or without varnish.

I remain, Reverend Father, your humble servant,
Rev. E. Bononcini.

The following correspondence of the *Boston Pilot* gives information that will delight many of my readers, who have taken much interest in this colony, since its inauguration in 1878:

St. Dominic's Colony, Kan.,
Rice Co., March 6th, 1882.

Editor of The Pilot.—The members of this colony are doing well, and in comfortable circumstances. Last year's crop has convinced our members that we have settled in a good part of Kansas, where we can make a comfortable living and save up a little money for a rainy day. Most of our neighbors realized from last

IN THE GREAT WEST. 51

year's wheat crop alone what paid for their land, with a good margin left, together with our favorable corn crop.

Some of our members are buying more land, which can be obtained on very easy terms from the Atchison, Topeka & Santa Fe Railroad Company.

Wheat has been selling since last harvest from $1.00 to $1.10 per bushel at our nearest market; corn brought from 50c. to 60c. per bushel. With these prices farmers can live and save money. Another sign of prosperity in our neighborhood is, my nearest neighbor has built himself a substantial frame house, and converted his original sod house into a stable. Others are preparing to do the same. Another sign of prosperity is the fact that all our farmers are going into stock-raising. I told you in my last letter, that I started here with one milch cow; we have now eight; also twelve other head of horned cattle, twenty in all.

Butter is bringing, now, twenty-two cents per pound in our nearest market. At that price it pays well to make butter for market.

The most energetic farmer in our locality is a man by the name of G. W. Fraizer, who according to his own story, settled here in 1878; his land being paid for, which was 160 acres. He commenced with one cow and forty-five dollars in money; he has now twenty milch cows, with thirty head of other horned cattle. Not having land enough, he bought eighty acres more a few months ago, for which he paid cash.

Francis and Patrick Finnan, two brothers, and members of the colony, say they would not go back to New York to live. They have bought more land. We have Mass every fourth Sunday in the month, given by Rev. Father Emmerich, who is very zealous in his pastoral duties. By the efforts of our beloved pastor we are to have a new church put up the coming spring; so I think we are doing as well as can be expected, both in spiritual and temporal blessings.

Weather splehdid for winter—stock doing well. Farmers have most of the tillable land all planted for next year's crops, which goes far to insure good yields. Two of our farmers have done exceedingly well the last year. Mr. Burnham, from eighty acres high prairie land, threshed recently 2,800 bushels of oats, and sold the crop for $1,400, and has an immense quantity of straw for cattle. Just to think of $1,400 worth of oats from eighty acres of land—double the value of the land in one crop! Another farmer, from the same kind of land, threshed 526½ bushels from thirteen acres, a still larger yield per acre.

Successful farming consists in obtaining the largest possible yield from the land used, not in planting over vast areas and raising ten bushels to the acre; fifty bushels, if grown from one acre are better than the same quantity from five acres. Farmers who take care of their poultry, and make that a part of the regular farm work, invariably reap good harvests from their labor. The poultry yard is a useful auxiliary to the successful farmer. The various trades and occupations depend in a greater or less degree upon the farmer for success in their different callings; and where will you find the professional man, the merchant, artisan, or mechanic, who can say he does not measure his success or failure in a greater or less degree by the prosperity or adversity of the farming community? I call attention to these things with a view to giving the best information available on a subject so important, not only to the people of this State, but to those of other countries, who look towards Kansas and who are eagerly discussing its resources and capabilities.

Probably few persons thoroughly comprehend the immense importance of the corn crop of this State, or realize its value. They little imagine that the corn produced in 1881 exceeds in value by one hundred per cent. that of the winter and spring wheat crops combined; or that it is not only the chief grain fed to our work animals, but the one wholly used to fatten a very large percentage of the animals slaughtered, or sold for slaughter, which in the last year were worth sixteen and a quarter million dollars.

Kansas is ahead, again, at the Cotton Exposition at Atlanta, Georgia. The Atchison, Topeka & Santa Fe Railroad Company's display took the prize for the "Best General Collection of Agricultural Products." This is something to be proud of; but we are ashamed of our last Legislature for failing to make some suitable provision for representation at that important exposition. The Atchison, Topeka & Santa Fe Railroad deserves, and will receive, the thanks of every Kansan for this additional evidence of their far-seeing enterprise. The exhibit made at Atlanta attracted attention generally throughout the South. The best time to come to Kansas is in the early fall and during the winter, so that preparations can be made for putting in an early crop. The prairie should be broken up so that the sod will be rotting during the winter. The time when new land is most easily broken is during the spring rains. This work ought not to be neglected, and preparations should be made for planting winter wheat, which should be in the ground about the first of

September. Early in the spring is a good time to come, say in the middle of February. Ground can be broken up and sod corn planted in April or May, and preparations made for planting winter wheat, with means to start on, and a due observation of the proper seed time and harvest, coupled with industry and economy, prosperity is certain, and a change from the old States or countries to Kansas must result in an increase of this world's goods.

JOHN TRAYNOR.

The following excellent letter is from the Rev. Ferdinand Wolf, O. S. B., from Southwestern Kansas:

VERY REV. FATHER:—In reply to your circular I cheerfully give you all information in my power regarding my district in Southwestern Kansas. I was sent here in May, 1878, and received part of Rev. Felix Swemberge's district, extending from Great Bend, Barton County, westward to the Colorado line, and from the Indian Territory to a line half-way between the Atchison, Topeka & Santa Fe R. R. It is 150 miles square. I have a church at Great Bend and at Windthorst, where I live; also St. Joseph Colony, both in Ford County. These three are my Sunday churches. And the Austrian Colony, eighteen miles northwest of Great Bend. I also visit several other places.

The lands in my district are of excellent quality. It is prairie land, partly rolling and partly level. The climate is so healthy that I have met at least 100 persons from the East who had been very sickly there and who are completely restored here, without either doctor or medicine. Water, pure and healthy, may be obtained everywhere by digging from ten to fifty feet. Only in exceptional cases further digging is required.

As far as I have been enabled to form an opinion entirely the best plan is to locate persons in colonies of at least 100 families. 120 or 140 families would be better still. Solitary settlers are often deprived of the consolations of religion for years; whereas a number of families living in the same vicinity soon contrive to get a church, a priest and a school. The chances for day-laborers are not good here. The supply of mechanics is quite equal to the demand. A capital of five hundred dollars is required to make a good start here. For people who have some means and are willing to work on a farm for some time there are certainly golden opportunities in the districts which you describe. I have been in Eastern Kansas and have seen many Irish people come there who had a hard time of it for a few years, owing to drought and other causes; but they persevered, and are now in good circumstances. Others became discouraged, left the place and lost their opportunities.

Land may be had here at $1.25 per acre from the government. The railroads charge more, but give longer time and some other considerations of value to settlers.

Truly yours,

FERDINAND WOLF,
O. S. B.

Spearville, Ford Co., Kan,
March, 1880.

JULY, 1883.

EXTRACTS FROM THE LATEST OFFICIAL PAMPHLET RELATING TO KANSAS.

By the kindness of Bishop Fink I have before me a pamphlet of sixty large pages, entitled "Kansas; its Resources and Capabilities," published this year, by the State Board of Agriculture. It is indeed pleasant to find that the carefully collected statistics contained in it more than confirm what has been written in the preceding description—some of which date as far back as 1880.

According to this authority we find the *wheat crop* of the State for 1882 to be 34,000,000 bushels, raised upon 1,465,000 acres, making the average per acre twenty-three and one-sixth bushels. The largest yield for one county is that of McPherson, in the central part of the State, in which 2,739,000 bushels were raised, averaging twenty-six bushels to the acre. The whole crop shows extraordinarily well for this State.

IN THE GREAT WEST.

The *corn crop* for the same year, 1882, is reported as follows: 157,000,000 bushels, raised on 4,442,000 acres, making the average yield thirty-five and one-third bushels to the acre. In 1870 the yield for the whole State was 16,700,000 bushels, and in 1875, 80,000,000 bushels. The immense value of the corn crop is well understood by all practical farmers in America. The oat crop has been 22,000,000 bushels, on 529,000 acres of land, making an average of forty-one and a half bushels to the acre.

But it is of more importance to my readers to know where and how a part of this fertile land may still be obtained.

Government land cannot be obtained generally in the eastern half of Kansas. Some of it, however, is still to be had. The following is a list of the offices and officers having charge of government land in 1883.

Arkansas Valley Land District.—Office at Larned, Pawnee Co. C. A. Morris, register; Henry Booth, receiver. Number of acres, 3,934,000.

Northern Land District.—Office at Oberlin, Decatur Co. A. L. Patchin, register; C. E. Chandler, receiver. Number of acres, over 3,000,000.

Northwestern Land District.—Office at Kerwin, Phillips Co. John Bissell, register; B. B. Hayes, receiver. Number of acres, about 120,000.

Osage Land District.—Office at Independence, Montgomery Co. M. I. Salter, register; H. M. Waters, receiver. Number of acres, about 250,000.

Salina Land District.—Office at Salina, Saline

Co. I. M. Hodge, register; H. S. Cunningham, receiver. Number of acres, about 15,000.

Western Land District.—Office at Wakeeney, Trego Co. B. I. F. Hamea, register; W. H. Pilkenton, receiver. Number of acres, about 2,500,-000.

Wichita Land District.—Office at Wichita, Sedgewick Co. R. L. Walker, register; James L. Dyer, receiver. Number of acres, 182,000.

Besides these lands there are in the State over a million acres of public school lands for sale, at an average of three dollars and fifteen cents an acre.

RAILROAD LAND.

Atchison, Topeka and Santa Fe R. R.—Headquarters, Topeka, Kansas. A. S. Johnson, land commissioner, to whom all inquiries should be addressed. This road has 1,850,000 acres still for sale, at prices ranging from one to twelve dollars an acre. There is very little at the latter price. The general average is three dollars an acre and eleven years time or less to suit purchaser.

Kansas Division Union Pacific R. R.—Headquarters, Kansas City, Mo. Land commissioner, B. McAllaster.

This very important corporation offer for sale 2,650,000 acres of land, at prices ranging between one dollar and fifty cents and ten dollars an acre. General average, four dollars per acre, on long time.

These roads offer many inducements to settle on

IN THE GREAT WEST. 57

their lands, all of which will be fully explained by application to the above named commissioners.

It is important to understand the full meaning of the expression "Government land," which so often occurs in all treatises relating to the West. It is not necessary to describe it in detail. Briefly, it means land, a valid title to which may be acquired by the mere fact of living upon it, and cultivating any part of it, for five years, the other conditions, which are very easy, being also fulfilled.

The title may be acquired in less than five years by the payment of a sum of money, not exceeding $2.50 an acre. In prairie countries it may be acquired, even without residence, in eight years, on the condition of planting a certain part of the land in trees.

COLORADO.

IF any proof were needed of the wonderful resources and progress of our western American States, it is abundantly furnished in the simplest recital of the history and present condition of the "Centennial" State. Colorado is so called because it was admitted as a sovereign State of our Union in the centennial year, 1876. The site of Denver, its beautiful capital, having a population now (1883) of about 50,000 souls, was occupied in 1858, by one cabin only; and no sign existed then of the coming city. True, the rush for gold to Pike's Peak in 1859, will explain, to some extent, this extraordinarily rapid growth; but the same growth is characteristic of the whole West after the completion of a few railroads. Dakota, for instance, gives proof of this fact, where we find a population of only 14,000 whites in 1870, and in 1880, 140,-000. Evidently the West is the true home of enterprise, industry and energy.

Colorado is an immense parallelogram. 375 miles long from east to west, and 275 miles wide from north to south. It is bounded north by Nebraska and Wyoming; east by Nebraska and Kansas; south by New Mexico and west by Utah. Its area is 104,000 square miles, or 66,880,000 acres. It is larger than New York and Pennsylvania; and three times as large as Ireland.

The surface of Colorado consists of three natural subdivisions of nearly equal size—the eastern section known as the "plains," the middle portion known as the mountains and mountain "parks," and the western section known as the slope of the great "interior basin." The "plains" may be described as a high, rolling table-land, from 4,000 to 6,000 feet above the level of the sea, well watered by many mountain streams with little woodland. The mountain region is generally about 125 miles wide, consisting of parallel and transverse ranges, which enclose four natural parks, each of which is as large as some of the older States of the Union. This mountain region occupies the whole middle part of the State from north to south. It has been so often and so graphically described by brilliant writers, that any attempt here at a true description of its magnificence would be out of place. The four "parks" may be briefly noticed, however. The "North Park" has a surface of 2,500 square miles, and is elevated 9,000 feet above the level of the sea. The "Middle Park" is 93 miles long by 60 miles wide, and has an area of 5,600 square miles. Lofty mountains surround this park on all sides, certain peaks of which attain a height of 14,500 feet. The "South Park" is 40 miles long and contains 1,200 square miles. From the summit of Mount Lincoln, on the west side of this park, and a few miles northeast of Leadville, more than two hundred mountain peaks may be descried. These are all from 12,000 to 14,000 feet in height. "San Louis Park," part of which lies in New Mexico, is larger than all of the three just noticed. No wonder, therefore, that Colorado has been called the "Switzerland" of America.

As to *timber*, we may say in general, that hard wood is almost entirely unknown. The principal wood consists of pine, spruce, larch, cottonwood and box elder. The timber line reaches to about 12,000 feet up the mountain sides. Fires often sweep through the forests; and trees are frequently prostrated by heavy winds.

The *rivers* of Colorado are, the Arkansas, which rises here, and has its head-waters near Mount Lincoln, 10,000 feet above the level of the sea; it has an eastwardly direction of 500 miles through the State, receiving several large streams in its course; the South Platte, with its numerous tributaries, drains the northeastern part of the State, and flows eastwardly into Nebraska. The western part of the State is drained into the Pacific Ocean and into the great interior basin.

THE SOIL AND CLIMATE

Of Colorado may now be briefly considered. The plains and parks *near* the water-courses, are fertile. Plains apparently sterile produce excellent crops, by means of irrigation. The explanation of this is that the good soil is covered with a surface of sand blown over it by high winds. Many parts of Colorado are found to be of no value for cultivation. There is a large amount of rich grazing land in all the State. In regard to climate it is reported, that snow falls as early as October, closing the mountain passes for the winter. A snow storm during the last days of March, has been three feet deep at Denver, and five feet in the nearest mountains. During two years the mercury ranged from 18 degrees below zero to 99 degrees above. The annual mean is 45 degrees. Notwithstanding the extremes of heat and cold, the exhilarating mountain air and splendid scenery, are making Colorado a favorite summer resort for tourists and invalids.

CHANCES FOR SETTLERS.

These may be noticed as follows: Agricultural productions, such as wheat, barley, oats, potatoes, and many of the principal garden vegetables prosper at an elevation of 7,000 feet above the sea level. The report of the wheat yield for 1877 is 1,700,000 bushels. This is certainly a good showing for what may be considered as a specifically mining country. It is needless to say that government land, amounting to millions of acres, may be procured all over the State. Railroad lands are also extensively in the market, at low prices and on long time. It becomes daily more and more apparent in this State, as in California and other mining States, that farming is, for a large number of the population, as profitable as mining.

The United States census report on the condition

of agriculture in Colorado in 1880, is as follows:—
Number of farms, 4,506 against 1,738 in 1870. Live
stock on farms in 1880: horses, 42,250; mules and
asses, 2,600; working oxen, 2,080; milch cows,
39,000; other cattle, 316,000; sheep, 750,000
(this item is worthy of note); swine, 8,000.

MINERALS AND MINING.

The State is principally known under this heading; and it takes the next highest place to California and Nevada in the production of the precious metals. Gold-mining began in 1858 and '59; Pike's Peak became what California had been ten years before. The yield of gold for the thirteen following years was estimated at sixty millions of dollars. For a few years there was a great falling off in mining industry; but the discovery of silver in immense quantities at Leadville and the surrounding mines, has made that section a centre of attraction for thousands of men during the last five years. The estimated bullion product of all Colorado for 1880, is fifteen millions of dollars. Accuracy, however, is impossible in this particular.

RAILROADS.

One of the most hopeful signs of permanent prosperity in this State, is the large number of railroads by which it is traversed—especially the eastern part. Ten years ago it was easy to count the number of miles of finished railroad here; now, Dec., 1882, it has reached the extraordinary figures of 2,500 miles.

IN THE GREAT WEST. 63

These roads generally enter Colorado from the east. They are, the Atchison, Topeka & Santa Fe; the Union Pacific (Kansas Division), the Union Pacific *proper*, and the Denver Pacific, which connects with the Union Pacific at Cheyenne, Wyoming Territory.* There are many other roads in the State, a knowledge of which is easily obtained by any one inclined to travel in this part of the country. So many fully equipped railroads in this new State furnish a sure guarantee of safe and rapid progress.

MANUFACTURING,

Except in connection with mining, is not yet developed to any great extent. The splendid water power of the State leaves no room to doubt that all kinds of manufacturing establishments will flourish here in course of time. At present they are mostly confined to flouring mills, quartz mills and lumber. The wages are nearly twice the average of the Eastern States; and this is true of all kinds of labor and housework, skilled or otherwise. The time from New York to Denver is from three to four days; and the fare, at first-class rates, about sixty dollars. Emigrant fare is half this amount. In 1880, by the census report, the number of manufacturing establishments was 600; hands employed, 5,000; capital invested, $4,300,000.

---

* One of the most important systems of railroad in all the West is the "Denver & Rio Grande." It is of immense value to this State; and it is giving very profitable employment to great numbers of workmen.

HISTORY AND POPULATION.

Vasquez Coronado, a Mexican explorer, entered this State in 1540, about the same time that the Mississippi river was discovered by DeSoto. Exploring expeditions were sent hither by the United States, under Lieut. Pike, in 1806; under Col. Long in 1820, and under the renowned explorer, John C. Fremont, in 1842. Only a few Mexicans and Spaniards, with some American trappers, hunters and traders, inhabited the country previous to the discovery of gold, in 1858. It became a Territory in February, 1861, and a State early in 1876. Hence, it is called the "Centennial" State.

The *Population* of Colorado, as shown by the census report of 1880, is as follows: Total, 194,327 (in 1870, 40,000); males 129,000; females 65,000; natives 154,500; foreigners 40,000; white 191,000; colored 2,500; Indians 154. Of the foreign population 8,800 were born in England; 8,234 in Ireland; 7,012 in the German Empire; 5,000 in Canada; 2,172 in Sweden; 1,673 in Scotland, and 1,212 in Wales.

Denver, the principal city and seat of government, is a place of wonderful growth, and is now the centre of five great railroads. Its population was (in 1880) 35,650.* *Leadville*, a city of only four years' growth, has a population of 14,800. It is about 11,000 feet above the level of the sea. There are several other cities and towns of from 5,000 to 10,000 people. It is not improbable that the entire

---
* It is 5,100 feet above tide water.

population of the State will have reached a million of souls in the next ten years.

THE CONDITION OF THE CATHOLIC CHURCH IN COLORADO.

The history of the Catholic Church, in Colorado, is marked in a special manner by the appointment of the RIGHT REV. JOSEPH PROJECTUS MACHEBEUF, a veteran missionary of the most self-sacrificing spirit, as Vicar Apostolic of the Territory, on the 16th of August, 1868. It is most cheering to see, by the Catholic Almanac of 1882, that there is probably not a single county in the State in which one or more churches, or at least a station, regularly attended, may not be found. It shows that, along with the rapid growth of the country in wealth and population, the "grain of mustard seed," that is, the Catholic faith, has indeed been planted, and its tender age carefully nurtured and wisely watched. The details are as follows: 1 Bishop, residing in Denver, 42 priests, 26 churches, 37 chapels, in which Mass is said occasionally, and 39 stations. There are five academies and several schools, three hospitals, and a Catholic population of 34,000 souls.

ADDITIONAL AND LATER FACTS.

I am just in receipt of the latest statistics in regard to the condition of the State, and am rejoiced to find that they more than confirm what has been written. The following extracts are chiefly taken from the *Colorado Tourist*, a beautiful and large pamphlet, which may be had *free* by writing for it to MR. THOMAS L. KIMBALL, Union Pacific R. R., Omaha, Nebraska. It is a valuable document:

TO BE JOTTED DOWN.

The name of Colorado is supposed to be derived from the many colored flowers and rocks. It means ruddy, florid.

The eastern part of the State (about 45,500 square miles) consists of plains ; the central part (32,000 square miles) mountains ; the western part (27,000 square miles) plateaux.

The total width of the mountains, in latitude of Middle Park, is seventy-five miles; in the latitude of South Park, 150 miles; and at the southern borders of the State, 180 miles.

The mean height of the State is about 7,000 feet; the lowest part of the State, at its eastern boundary, is but little over 3,000 feet, while the highest peak is 14,400 feet.

The average elevation of the plains above tide-water is 6,000 feet. They are drained by the South Platte, Arkansas, and Republican rivers and branches.

The foot-hills have an average elevation of 8,000 feet. "Timber line" (the highest point at which timber grows), is from 11,000 to 12,000 feet.

In the twenty years Colorado has been producing gold and silver, her mines have yielded over $100,000,000 worth of ore. The yield for 1879 was nearly $20,000,000.

The Colorado newspapers put down the yield of the mines for 1880 at $40,000,000 to $50,000,000.

The farming area of Colorado is estimated at 5,000,000 acres. Of these lands only about 90,000 acres are now actually under cultivation.

When in Colorado the reader should visit Estes Park, Middle Park, North Park, South Park, Idaho Springs, Manitou, Georgetown, Brookvale, Boulder, Central, Fort Collins, Colorado Springs, and as many other pleasure and health resorts as time will permit.

HEALTH IN COLORADO.

The following brief extract conveys as much sound sense and good advice as one will be likely to meet with in so small a space, though he look about "all summer:"

Manitou is a "healthy resort," as are several other places in Colorado, and it may briefly be said, and with all seriousness, that the Centennial State, while it is no more of a cure-all than the patent nostrums of the period, can indeed afford blessed relief, and life itself, to many a forlorn and despairing sufferer. "Words," says the Chinese proverb, "may deceive, but the eye cannot play rogue;" and one may see men and women walking about and using and enjoying life, who long ago, if they had staid in the East, would have, in Western parlance, "gone over the range," or joined the great majority.

"Why, they keep me here for an example of the effects of the climate," said a worthy business man at Colorado Springs. "I came here from Chicago on a mattress."

And so did many others, and so may many, many more, if they will only display ordinary common sense, and heed a few plain words of advice, which will surely have the indorsement of those who know the country well.

They should, firstly, on no possible account (and this caution is disregarded every day), think of coming until they have sent to some respectable, responsible and experienced physician, resident in Colorado, not their own crude ideas of their condition, but a diagnosis prepared by a doctor who knows them well.

They should, secondly, make up their minds that the climate may *arrest* disease without curing it, and that a permanent residence may be indispensable.

They should, thirdly, be prepared for a careful life, largely out-door, and abandon, once for all, any ideas of the working of miracles in their cases, or of the propriety of disregarding the great laws of health in Colorado, any more than in New York or Memphis.

OFFICIAL REPORT OF MINING IN THE UNITED STATES FOR THE YEAR 1882.

COLORADO HEADS THE LIST.

Our Gold and Silver Product in 1882.—While our gold and silver mines show a very satisfactory yield last year ($89,300,000) it is noticeable that California, once the chief mining State, has declined to the second in the list, yielding precedence to Colorado. The leading Territories and States, with their respective yields, are:

Colorado, $19,850,000; California, $17,645.000; Nevada, $8,750,000; Utah, $6,950,000; Montana, $6,920,000; Idaho, $8,500,000; Dakota, $3,475,000; Arizona, $8,565,000. Of the total product $32,500,000 was gold, and $46,800,000 silver. Nevada shows a decline of $1,500,000 as compared with the year before—a fact attributed to the approaching exhaustion of the Comstock lode. California's decline in mining wealth is more than compensated for in its thrifty progress in the production of grain, fruit and wine; but there is no such recompense in Nevada, and that little State seems doomed to decay. Of the whole silver product $15,750,000 was exported, less than one-third. Nearly all the territories are steadily increasing their yield, and it seems probable that the country will long continue to augment its stock of gold and silver.

The special attention of farmers and farm laborers is called to the following account of a recent work on Colorado, published by Orange Judd, of New York. This review of the book and abridgment of its contents is from the *Boston Herald* of January 10th, 1883:

FARMING IN COLORADO.

How Smart Men May Make a Living There. Irrigation the Secret of Agricultural Prosperity.

One naturally thinks of Colorado as a mining, more than an agricultural State, and the general impression that it is pre-eminently a field for the man of the pick rather than for the man of the plough is undoubtedly correct. And yet farming in Colorado is profitable. The State lies so far away from the chief agricultural commonwealths, and its mining industry creates a profitable home market right at the farmer's door, that tilling the ground is a paying occupation. Mr. William E. Pabor, the author of a book just published, entitled "Colorado as an Agricultural State" (Orange Judd & Co.), gives a deal of interesting information regarding the Rocky Mountain commonwealth. He has written his book to answer two questions likely to be asked by those persons who think of settling in Colorado—"Is Colorado a farming country?", and "Does it pay to farm in Colorado?" Mr. Pabor says: "As compared with Illinois, Minnesota. Nebraska or Kansas, Colorado is not a farming country. The breadth of land suitable for cultivation is limited, and the condition of the climate peculiar. As in the days when the boys in blue met the boys in gray upon the battle field, there was a 'dead line,' passing which meant danger and death, so in the agricultural field of Colorado there is a 'water line,' to go beyond which, means disappointment and destruction to the stalwart sons of the soil who seek to gain a livelihood from the bosom of Mother Earth. Inside the line, certain conditions being complied with, success is certain."

The farmer going from the East to Colorado, has much to unlearn. It is better to abandon all notions and begin anew. Dependent upon irrigation for the growth of his crops, he must study the methods and meet the requirements of the climate. One great point to be thought of in considering Colorado as a place of settlement, is the excellent home market which the farmer has. The danger of an over-supply of cereals, fruits and vegetables is not, says Mr. Pabor, among the possibilities of the future. Over $10,000,000 worth of agricultural products are shipped every year into the State. The land that lies where water can overrun it and permeate it is valuable land, and will, at no far-distant day, bring prices that would now seem wild and extravagant to name. Agriculture in Colorado and the valley lands being inseparable, they must be taken together in considering the amount of land available for cultivation, and locations where water can be obtained.

The days of pioneering in the valleys of the Cache-la Poudre, the St. Vrain and Boulder are over. Improved farms, cultivated homes abound. The man who comes with money can easily find the man who is willing to sell his farm for money. To the farmer who comes with but little money, there are occasional opportunities in Northern Colorado, and abundant ones in the southern and western part of the State to secure farms partly improved.

Mr. Pabor's chapter on "Irrigation" and "The Measurement of Water," will be read with instruction by anyone wishing to gain a knowledge of the system of irrigation which obtains on the eastern slope of the Rockies. The chapter is one which it would be difficult to condense into the space of a newspaper article, and an understanding of it is better to be had by the assistance of engravings. It is estimated that there are in Colorado 5,000,000 acres of land which may be irrigated. Eleven-twelfths of the irrigable land of the State await settlement.

It is thought by many, says the author, that irrigation is a very expensive method. This belief, no doubt, keeps many farmers from settling in Colorado. But it is not true. On the contrary, it is rather an advantage to "hold the rain in the hollow of one's hand." It may add a little to the labor required to be performed on an acre of ground, but the increased yield more than repays this extra toil. The cultivation of crops being insured by the ability to apply the moisture just when it is needed, drouth is defied and a harvest is almost certain.

The preparation of irrigating canals will not on an average, exceed the expense of drainage required in rainy countries, while a dry country means dry air, health, clear skies and good roadways. Wheat can be raised at an expense of 50 cents per bushel, or $10 per acre, taking the low average of twenty bushels as the yield, leaving a net profit of $14 per acre. Oats can be raised at an expense of $10, and yield a profit not lower than wheat. Corn can be raised at a cost of $7 per acre, leaving a profit of $14. Potatoes average in expense $20, and in moderately good seasons return a profit of $60 per acre. It will be seen that a good margin of profit lies in these figures, and, while there may be seasons when excessive drouth, or untimely frost, or grasshopper visitations may curtail the harvest, yet these are less frequent than the storms, the drouth and the insects that periodically visit the fields in the Eastern States.

In his chapter on questions and answers, Mr. Pabor gives a vast deal of information in a very condensed form. He advises against any family man coming to Colorado without cash. Let us quote a few passages:

"How much money ought a young man to have?"

"A young man with $300 in his possession when he reaches Colorado, can easily secure a foothold, and eventually become a landowner."

"How much ought a married man to have?"

"If with a small family, he should at least have $500. With an economic management, indoors and out, this will secure land, a cabin and subsistence for the first six months."

"When is the best time to come?"

"In the fall, for the preparatory work of moving,

getting settled and preparing for the spring work should not be put off until the sowing season comes."

"What is the general nature of the soil."

"A sandy loam predominates, though a stiff clay is occasionally met with. It is very easy to work, and only requires common attention to return a thousandfold."

"What can be raised in Colorado?"

"Almost everything. Wheat, corn, barley, rye, amber cane, vegetables of all sorts, fruits of nearly every kind common in our latitude."

In chapters on agriculture, fruit-growing, and cattle and sheep, Mr. Pabor turns aside from farming proper and gives a deal of information of use to the intending immigrant. He discusses the artesian well question, and is of the opinion that these wells will be of incalculable benefit to the State. The movement to sink artesian wells in Colorado is one of great interest. If successful, hundreds of thousands of acres will be changed from merely wild pasture land to arable land, capable of producing thirty bushels of wheat to the acre. Once establish the fact that artesian wells can be sunk on the prairies, and a stride forward will be made in the agriculture of Colorado which will put it in the front rank of grain-producing areas.

www.ingramcontent.com/pod-product-compliance
Lightning Source LLC
Chambersburg PA
CBHW020247090426
42735CB00010B/1861